NATIONAL GEOGRAPHIC

School Publishing

D0584324

Star Sightings

PIONEER EDITION

By Beth Geiger

CONTENTS

Star Sightings

By Beth Geiger

Have you ever seen a really starry night?
It's out of this world!

Counting Stars. Altogether, there are 88 official constellations

Starry Nights

Stars are huge fiery balls of gases in space. They are so far away that they look tiny—except for one star, our sun! It looks big. It's the closest star to Earth.

Some stars are big and bright. Others are very dim. A few even have colors, like red or blue. On a clear night, there are too many stars to count. You can see thousands with just your eyes. But take a peek through a telescope. There are millions more.

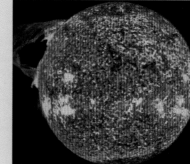

Ball of Fire. Our sun is a star.

Connect the Dots

From here on Earth, some stars seem to form patterns. One pattern looks like the letter *W*. Another looks like a giant bear.

These shapes are **constellations**. People have noticed them for a long time. There are even stories about them.

Star Party

Constellations only exist in people's imaginations. In space, the stars in a constellation are not that close to each other. They just look that way from Earth.

Let's meet some of the most famous constellations in the sky.

The Big Dipper

The most famous constellation in the sky is the Big Dipper. Three bright stars form the handle. Four more stars make the bowl.

   This star pattern is easy to recognize. If you live north of the equator, you can see it all year.

Little Dipper

Polaris

Big Dipper

Polaris Points the Way

Sailors in the old days were very happy to see the Big Dipper. It was like a map. It helped sailors find their way home.

How? The two stars that form the back of the Big Dipper's bowl point to another star called Polaris. Polaris is also called the North Star.

Polaris never moves. It stays in one place while other stars seem to rotate around it. So sailors knew that if they could find it, they would always know which way was north.

Night Guide. For hundreds of years sailors have used Polaris to find their way.

Polaris ⟶

Orion: The Hunter

Orion is probably the most popular constellation. Orion is shaped like a hunter. The easiest part of Orion to see is his belt. It's three perfectly matched stars in a line. Orion also has a bow and arrow. A sword hangs from his belt. He looks ready for action!

Cassiopeia: Queen of the Sky

The ancient Greeks said that Cassiopeia was a queen. But to most of us, this constellation looks more like a big *W*. Some people think it looks like a throne. Maybe if you squint you can imagine a queen.

According to legend, Cassiopeia bragged to the sea gods. She said that her daughter was prettier than theirs. Big mistake. The gods didn't like that! To punish her, they sent her into the sky. And there she sits.

Cassiopeia A

Kaboom!

About 300 years ago, one of the five stars in Cassiopeia exploded. That star, Cassiopeia A, became a **supernova**. A supernova is the dusty, gassy remains of an old star. Through a telescope, supernovas look a bit like colorful clouds. Modern **astronomers** can even see a piece of the old star.

ready to spring. Of course, the lion is imaginary. His body, feet, tail, and head are stars.

Leo is one of many constellations shaped like an animal. There is Taurus the Bull. There are horses, dogs, fish, and birds. There's even a unicorn!

Does Leo look like a lion to you? Many people think it does.

Sly Cat. Some think the Egyptian sphinx was based on the constellation Leo.

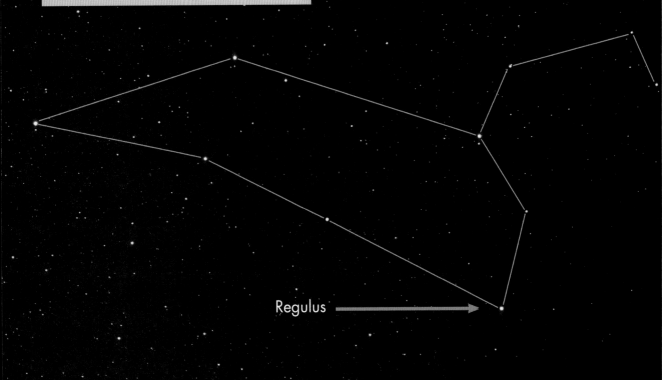

Regulus ⟶

Super Spinner

Leo's brightest star is called Regulus. Regulus is part of the lion's front legs.

Like other stars, Regulus spins. In fact, Regulus spins super fast.

Astronomers say that if Regulus spun any faster, it could spin itself to pieces!

Scorpius: A Real Grabber

Watch out! This constellation looks real enough to sting. It resembles a real scorpion. It even has a long, curved stinger.

Legends say that Scorpius stung Orion to death. That's why they never appear near each other. Scorpius appears in the summer. Orion appears in the winter.

Antares

Good Night, Star Bright!

Scorpius has a big heart. That heart is a bright star called Antares.

Antares is a **red supergiant** star. Red supergiants are the largest stars there are.

Stars have life cycles. And red supergiants are old. When they die, they explode big time! What's left is a supernova.

Wordwise

astronomer: a scientist who studies the planets, stars, and galaxies

constellation: a pattern of stars

red supergiant: a large, dying star

supernova: the remains of an exploded star

The Milky Way

Big and Bigger

We live on the planet Earth. Earth revolves around a star, our very own sun. It seems hard to imagine anything bigger than the sun.

But the sun is part of something far, far bigger. That something is a galaxy called the Milky Way. In the Milky Way, there are billions of other stars like our sun!

Starry Spiral

You can't really see something if you are inside it. But astronomers have seen other galaxies through their telescopes. From that, they have a good idea of what the Milky Way looks like.

The galaxy looks like a giant, flat spiral. The spiral shape is because it is spinning. Our sun is in one of the Milky Way's spiral arms.

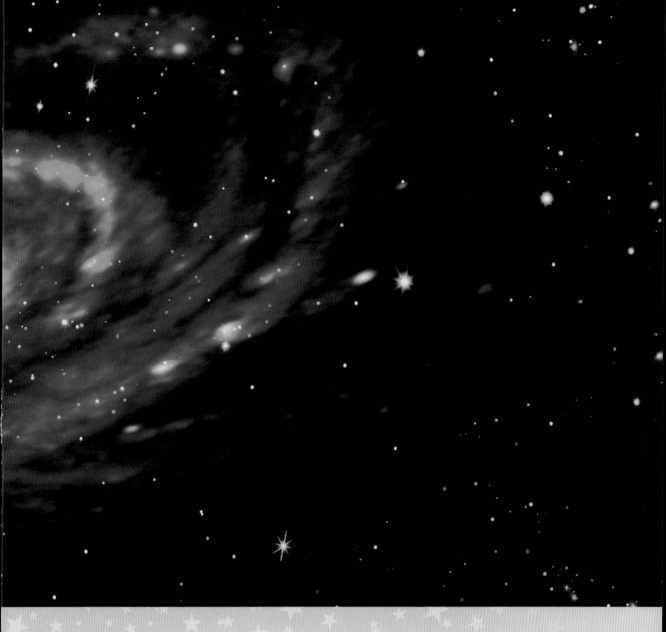

On a Spiral Arm

You can't see all of the Milky Way. But sometimes you can see part of it. Think of a Frisbee tipped on edge. That's how the Milky Way looks from Earth.

Pick a really clear, dark night. Now, look for a dense band of stars across the sky. That's our galaxy—from inside it! This sight will leave you star struck.

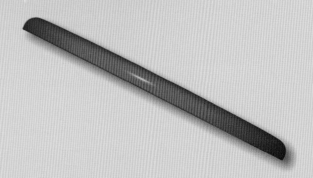

Amazing View. From Earth, the Milky Way looks like a line, just like this Frisbee tipped on its side.

Stars

Let's see how much you've learned about star sightings.

1 How do stars look different from each other?

2 What are constellations?

3 How did sailors use Polaris?

4 What stars are the largest stars there are?

5 What does the Milky Way look like in the night sky?